Title : 87 Not Out
Author : Stuart Bonnington
ISBN: 978-0-6458923-0-7

©2023 Stuart Bonnington
The moral rights of the author have been asserted.

Leunig cartoons reproduced by permission.

Edit & Design:
PB Publishing
Gisborne Victoria 3437

Printed in Australia
by IngramSpark, Dandenong, Victoria.

ACKNOWLEDGEMENTS

With thanks to Michael Leunig for his generous permission to reproduce cartoons; with thanks for the quotes sourced from various poems and books; and with special thanks for the huge unending support from Jay.

CONTENTS

Introduction • 1

1 Musings • 3

2 Appreciation • 5

3 Observations • 9

4 Wisdom • 14

5 Friends • 19

6 Family • 27

7 Personal dislikes and heroes • 38

8 Useful any more? • 43

9 General thoughts on life and love • 51

10 Commerce and life today • 57

11 Employment • 63

12 Loneliness • 68

13 Ill health • 76

14 Music • 81

15 Bemused and appalled • 85

16 Routines traditions and democracy • 89

17 Women • 93

18 Ownership • 98

19 Politics • 102

20 The now • 106

21 Ambitions • 110

Cross my heart, I remember when common sense was delivered to the door, each morning by horse and cart —

Completely undebated, was common sense — unprocessed you might say: full of organisms and rough seeds; it's what the body needs.... you could feel it do you good.

You have to go through so much these days — crawl across a field of broken bottles — half a life of suffering and sin — be done over and done in.....

Equally to the rich and poor. What a bold start it was to find it sitting there on the porch — all yours, fresh as a daisy and as good as gold.

How could such a useful thing — so plentiful back then yet so revered — become so lost and rare; and so WEIRD?

...Before you find it once again. Perhaps one morning — on the porch and in the sun of early spring — lo and behold — on the step — thank Christ! — a little common sense is there again.

Leunig

INTRODUCTION

This is a follow up to my previous book 'What's It All About'. This is a Book 2—now that I am over 87!

When you get to my age, the great dilemma is, "To whom do you address this 'revelatory insight'?" There are so many subjects and areas of the unknown that even posing the question 'Why'? makes me feel guilty of an arrogance for going near the fringe of luck.

What has changed from the 'Old' me that wrote, 'What's it all About'? in 2020?

When I first thought about another book, the idea was a new and updated autobiography. That inclination did not last long as I have not achieved much of note in recent times. However, I have succeeded if even it only applies to my longevity.

Thus, it has become a 'Memoir of Musings'. This is much easier because I can describe myself as 'free spirited and over 21'. That immediately gives a clue to some of my opinions and attitudes but, I hasten to add, I hope they are not prejudices.

1
MUSINGS

"About the time one learns how to make the most of life, most of it has gone!"

I have always loved poetry thanks to excellent exposure at my secondary school by my English Master, Mr (aka Butch) Goldie Brown. He had earned an MA and many other degrees.

A famous sonnet (Sonnet 23) written by John Milton around 1650 when blindness was approaching him, epitomises many of the thoughts that have crystalised now in my mind.

On his Blindness (John Milton)

When I consider how my light is spent
Ere half my days, in this dark world and wide
And that one talent which is death to hide
Lodg'd with me useless, though my soul more bent
To serve therewith my Maker, and present
My true account, lest he returning chide,
"Doth God exact day-labour, light denied?"
I fondly ask. But Patience, to prevent

> *That murmur, soon replies, "God doth not need*
> *Either man's work or his own gifts: who best*
> *Bear his mild yoke, they serve him best. His state*
> *Is Kingly; thousands at his bidding speed*
> *And post o'er land and ocean without rest:*
> *They also serve who only stand and wait."*

This wonderful poem was written a long time ago when godliness was important and whether individuals had been put on earth for a specific purpose was questioned. It was a big world that awaited God's commands.

The thoughts evoked are still important if not quite so pertinent. It was suggested that Milton was prone to dreams and hallucinations when blindness began to encroach on his life. The word oneiric (relating to dreams and dreaming) has also been attached to his famous Sonnet 23. The poem certainly epitomises some of my thoughts as I become an older person. When you are over 87, how different are things?

Most things are now in my mind, and that is pleasing because actually achieving is not so important. The pleasure comes from the considering. Being contemplative. Contented, more philosophical.

2.
APPRECIATION

My mind is a huge new area for appreciation.

What's it all about? Seems to me to be a world of wonderment. Everyone has a bucket list of things to do and places to go. Imagination can contribute to satisfaction in some, or most, of these areas.

The mind is such a resource. More and more I have admiration for my mind. It is so clever because amongst other things it allows me to keep some of my opinions totally to myself!

The old 'ambition bogey' seems to have receded as I roam freely over everything and anything. I really do seem to have all aspects covered. My mind seems so versatile.

The ego is buried! Freedom of speech, behaviour and attitude is a given in our democracy. As is sung in many songs **and is a mantra of modern psychology,** "Let it all out"!

Service to others has always been a part of my being, when and how I could afford it both in time and money. It was reflected in my long membership in the Rotary organisation. I was recruited a long time ago when the rules and habits of society were very different from today. On and off I have been a Rotarian for over 50 years, from my first club in early 1960. Back

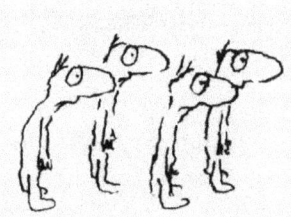

then, potential members were researched anonymously before being informed and invited, and then only after a home visit and several preliminary discussions! Members could only be males then. With hindsight and changing times it all now sounds so silly.

Rotary is far from that now, and rules and regulations are more up to date and reflective of our society. It is a successful and respected worldwide service club with no gender or racial barriers, appreciating the input of talented women.

I am currently not a Rotarian because of current inflexibility for membership, on a part-time basis, of more than one club. When that changes, I will perhaps reapply to re-enter a world of fellowship and enjoyment under the basic principle, "is it fair to all concerned?"

In my mind I can be controversial and often I query what seems to me to be the ridiculous. For example, my opinion on how the Essendon Football Club in Melbourne handled the recruitment of a new President—appointing and then quickly withdrawing the appointment (of a well qualified ex-CEO) after a particuar religious connection was revealed—may be at odds with many others, and makes me somewhat critical of how far our society has not really advanced relative to bigotry.

This recent debacle defies common sense to me, and I question the wisdom of the parties involved. Surely, in this day and age of tolerance and public exposure, the ability to perform a role without racial or homophobic bigotry can be expected. I really do shudder at such an appalling consequence.

People do not need to get agitated over some small road misdemeanour as they drive home to enjoy the evening.

The search for more meaning in an unhurried way, not constantly but consistently.

If there is a life here after, come back as an eagle? (And maybe a few other things?)

3
OBSERVATIONS

"Real unselfishness consists in sharing in the interests of others"
— Santayana

One more piece of poetry, or in fact lyrics to a song, called *Both Sides Now*—I have always called it "Clouds". Selected verses in it I find significant. It is a famous song by Joni Mitchell, better enjoyed by me when sung by Judy Collins,

> "Rows and flows of angel hair
> And ice cream castles in the air
> And feather canyons everywhere,
> I've looked at clouds that way
>
> But now they only block the sun
> They rain and snow on everyone
> So many things I would 've done
> But clouds got in the way
>
> I've looked at clouds from both sides now
> From up and down and still somehow
> It's cloud illusions, I recall
> I really don't know clouds at all."

WHAT IS THIS LIFE?

LIFE IS A HOLIDAY ON EARTH.

The accommodation is a bit unusual but it's clean and comfortable — it's your body, quite a good base for an existence.

"I'LL JUST PERSONALISE IT AND IT WILL FEEL LIKE HOME"

LIFE IS AN INTERESTING PLACE TO VISIT; QUITE ENJOYABLE AND WELL WORTH THE EXPERIENCE BUT YOU WOULDN'T WANT TO BE THERE TOO LONG. YOU WOULD ALWAYS FEEL LIKE A BIT OF AN OUTSIDER.

You arrive at your holiday destination and there, to meet you, wearing a big smile, is your host and guide.

"HELLO, I'M YOUR MUM; I'LL GET YOU STARTED AND SHOW YOU AROUND. WOULD YOU LIKE SOME MILK?"

YOU STUDY SOME MAPS, GO FOR A BIT OF AN EXPLORE AND SOON YOU'RE GETTING THE HANG OF IT. THE PLACE IS FULL OF HOLIDAY MAKERS AND BEFORE TOO LONG YOU'RE HAVING A HOLIDAY ROMANCE! AND WHY NOT?!

HOLIDAYS ON EARTH CAN BE WONDERFUL AND HORRIBLE, BUT REGARDLESS, IT'S ALWAYS A BIT SAD WHEN THEY COME TO AN END. AND ALWAYS A GOOD FEELING TO KNOW THAT YOU'RE RETURNING HOME TO WHERE YOU REALLY BELONG; ALL REFRESHED AND WITH SOME LOVELY HOLIDAY MEMORIES.

Leunig

(For brevity and because it suits me, I now leave out three verses.)

> "Tears and fears and feeling proud
> To say "I love you" right out loud
> Dreams and schemes and circus crowds
> I've looked at life that way
>
> But now old friends are acting strange
> They shake their heads; they say I've changed
> Well, something's lost, but something's gained
> In living every day
> I've looked at life from both sides now
> From win and lose and still somehow
> It's life's illusions, I recall
> I really don't know life at all
>
> I've looked at life from both sides now
> From up and down, and still somehow
> It's life's illusions, I recall
> I really don't know life at all."

Very pertinent. The significance and emphasis changes through the song from 'clouds' to reference to 'life.'

The most important thing for me is being aware of the world. These can be perceptions, and realities. The sensory organs are mainly closeted deep inside a dark and protected cranium so they often miss the illusions or magic. They need help and encouragement.

As a regular early morning walker I watch others and observe their manners. Eighty per cent give a happy 'good morning' or similar greeting, ten per cent grunt, ten per cent ignore others.

We need humour in our lives. However, I acknowledge many people have problems.

Don't get out of bed on the wrong side, or worry about having been dealt a 'bad hand.' Try to always be positive.

Companion animals have a major role to play—cats, dogs, horses are as far as I go, but the pleasure animals bring into most families is undeniable. Mine also.

Real and Miscellaneous Observations

Are these the Cartoons of Life? See the Leunig cartoons, (each chapter has an appropriate cartoon from Leunig, with formal permission).

For most problems there is always another way to try to resolve it.

A touch of humour is a great aid and so I add some of my favourites. These can be applied commercially, privately, physically, or attitudinally.

Look for the sunshine! Be positive and have some fun. Try to be interesting to others. Give it a go! Be curious in all things.

Now I have learnt to be a contributor in conversation, but try not to dominate.

I do appreciate I have been lucky enough to have enjoyed physical fitness that has allowed me to continue a regime of exercise that includes tennis weekly, and often if somewhat irregularly, some gym work that varies over walking, bicycling, rowing, and light weights.

When I was considering this book, I had thought I would

spend hours eavesdropping in coffee shops and the like, as I mentally and then actually recorded the regular and often repeated little gems of wisdom that came over shared 'coffee and muffins.' Many of those follow in a later chapter: mild, mad, or just silly.

Just remember, whatever you think of some of the 'sillies', tomorrow is another day. Illustration: Our eyes are placed in the front because it is more important to look ahead than to look back.

"The human mind should be like a good hotel—open the year around." — William Lyon Phelps.

4

WISDOM

"An old man forfeits one of the greatest human rights; no longer is he judged by his peers." — Goethe

So today I am no longer judged as I was as a young person. It fills me full of wonderment that so many of today's young people have as much appreciation and are as wise as us 'oldies'—we who have taken a lifetime to accumulate the wisdom. Of course, some kids are crass, but so are many 'oldies' who have been at it all their lives.

A very wise saying attributed to one of the tennis coaches Serena Williams used was that for success, "You need composure, clarity, and commitment."

Aquarius — The Water Bearer
As an Aquarian I was always drawn to this Zodiac sign and what it meant. The most powerful item in life. Water!
   What a mix of personality traits. Aquarians are usually associated with water but air-related concepts must be added to that. Aquarians are considered innovative, progressive, and

87 NOT OUT

often involved in planning revolutions. I hope in a little way I have some of that.

My own feeling has always been influenced by the concept of a water carrier, the mystic healer, who bestows water, or life, upon the land. More relevant perhaps in Australia more than New Zealand, my place of birth.

Personality wise, I am more inclined to be described as a 'rebel at heart', my daughter giving me a big wooden spoon many years ago, and yet I have always enjoyed team building and the leadership associated with achieving the established goals—though sometimes prepared to break the rules if they seemed petty or non-productive. Sometimes I can be distant in relationships.

I have a love for the blue of the sea, the sound and sight of the waves, the beautiful blue of a clear blue sky, the sound of the wind when I am in good shelter, and the always changing sight of the outdoors, and I regularly look at and admire clouds. I love being outside.

I have a huge bank of appreciation for my Aunty Meg, as from the time I was 10 years old, I spent a lot of time on holidays with her. Aunty Meg always found the time to take me down to Thorns Beach in Takapuna, Auckland, (a little beach between Takapuna and Milford) allowing me to simply climb over the rocks looking for crabs and letting the wind buffet me. She also taught me how to swim.

It was Meg who first alerted me to the wonderful and lengthy poem, *The Rime of the Ancient Mariner*, by Samuel Taylor Coleridge. I think her point then was generally more about salt water and the oceans than what was later emphasised to me in the days of my education; studying what it all meant in one of the longest poems ever composed about inner struggles. Coleridge (1772-1834) seems very relevant today with a high proportion of the ever-growing population of our world with complex mental health problems; also, our world perhaps unable in the future to find enough clean fresh water to survive on.

From *The Rime of the Ancient Mariner*:

> "Water, Water everywhere nor any drop
> to drink,
> And all the boards did shrink
> Water, water, everywhere".

I thought the poem pertinent. Wars are currently, and in future will continue to be, fought over water.

For example, the CWMI (Composite Water Management Index) report states that in India, by 2030 the demand for water will be twice the available supply. In Africa every day more than 360,000 children die from diahorrhea attributed to poor water and sanitation. The statistics roll on and on. Predictions about world wars over water are not so exaggerated.

For the world's poor there is no 'beauty is in the eye of the beholder', and the maxim 'Tomorrow is another day' does not apply.

"*Common-sense is an uncommon degree, is what the world calls wisdom*". — Coleridge

I think it important to judge a person also by their considered questions rather than just by their answers. Surely common sense is a major part of wisdom.

This is where I stray into a hot topic, but with the abortion rights legal issue currently raging in the USA, it seems basic to me that women have the right to control their own destiny and have responsibility for their own bodies.

5

FRIENDS

"Mere family never made a man great. Thought and deed, not pedigree, are the passports to enduring fame." — Skobeleff

Friends are so important in the full deep meaning of life.

These are my non-family friends. There are only three people, who are all now regretfully deceased.

(a) Geoffrey John Burton

Geoff started at the Shell Company where we both started out with one another, as trainee executives. Maybe as the mail boys! We had no accountability, and had huge fun as we drove the Accountant and most of the other staff crazy with our irresponsible attitudes and fun. Geoff had more humour in one finger than I had in my whole body. Everyone, I mean everyone, just loved him, including my then girlfriend Ngaire, who later became my first wife.

Socially and workwise, Geoff was well respected. He was a fanatical rugby player and became a stalwart all his adult life of the College Rifles Football Club. He was also an excellent

STUART BONNINGTON

THE SMILE

I shot a smile into the air
It came to earth I know not where;
Perhaps on someone elses face
In some forgotten, quiet place.

Perhaps somewhere a sleeping child
Has had a happy dream and smiled
Or some old soul about to die
Has smiled and made a little sigh;

Has sighed a simple, final prayer
Which lifts up gently in the air
And flows into the world, so wild,
Perhaps to wake the sleeping child.

leunig

tennis player with a home court. He had such a silly sense of humour which included throwing epileptic fits at parties, much to the chagrin for a moment of some attendees. Of course, not politically correct at all today. He excelled at ringing friends and leaving silly messages to ring and ask for 'Mr Lyon' or similar at the Zoo. Of course, childish, but then such good social fun. Geoff had a foot deformity that seriously handicapped his mobility in sport but he never emitted a word of complaint or disappointment.

It was a huge pleasure for Ngaire and me for Geoff to officiate at our wedding and for him to remain a close friend over the years as our family grew, and long after I left Shell, where he remained. 'Uncle Geoff' was a permanent family friend to our children.

Geoff was a keen mountaineer and country hill cyclist and when he had a serious accident over the handlebars of his bike much of his physical activities were curtailed. However, the more serious physical impediments to his lifestyle never impaired his cheerful self.

I still miss his friendship, silly sense of humour and all the experiences that totalled more than 50 years.

(b) John Orr

John and I worked for Milne and Choice Ltd (M&C), a prominent department store in Queen Street, Auckland, many years ago. M&C had just announced they were opening a new satellite store in the suburb of New Lynn. It had been announced that I was to be the new manager; I was 26 years of age, and we were appointing all the staff (old and new) for the store.

One day I was descending on the escalator to the ground floor and a voice called, "Mr Bonnington?" as relationships then were quite formal. I replied, "Yes" and wondered who this little bloke with a slight Scottish accent was.

"I'm John Orr and I have been appointed your Assistant Manager at Lynn Mall. Can we have a coffee?" It was one of the luckiest days of my life.

We had about two months getting to know each other while the new store and shopping centre were being completed. We had the privilege of mainly selecting our own staff of around forty who we needed and wanted to be able to build a happy team. We controlled nine departments and a mezzanine coffee shop. A hairdressing salon also on the mezzanine was controlled from Head Office in Queen Street.

John was gay, and his partner worked for the opposition store FTC. There was never any conflict. John had served in the British Army in the Second World War, and his favourite story (amongst the many) was how when the war ceased, he had finished up in Paris for a few days directing traffic. He thought it hilarious; a short (5' 7") Scot directing traffic on the wrong side of the street as a two-stripe corporal!

John had a description of one of our buyers who he very much admired, and with whom he closely worked, and who had also served in the war as an officer. John used to say "He is the type you wanted in the trenches because of the now popular saying;

'I've got your back'!" John himself was utterly dependable, and I grew to know that was how we related in our work.

God forbid if a couple of smart gung-ho 'smart alecs' ever cast aspersions about his sexuality. He could stand up for himself. My friendship and respect for John developed and extended right through to his funeral.

John became a long-time favourite friend of Ngaire, and our two children Dene and Lianne. Perhaps it is necessary for friends to become "family friends" to enter the special number 1 category. Remarkably, John never held a driver's licence so we went many places together with me driving. He regularly accused me of trying to be racing car driver 'Fangio'!

Running a department store and being responsible for more than forty staff seemed a big job to me then, but today in retrospect it seems tiny, when later in South Africa I controlled the destinies of over 400 staff. A lesson that everything is always in perspective?

The 'getting to know' the M&C team happened often on a Friday night, after retail closing time but before lock up and lights out) as we sat around and chatted over a beer or wine. As part of team building we had invented 'the oyster run'. Much fun to purchase bags of said shellfish and distribute to staff.

I was happy in my role and was surprised to be invited into the Rotary Club of New Lynn, a club of around fifty members. It was a small acknowledgement of work being done with handicapped children. This then was an honour and gave a fillip to my leadership profile.

I learned so much about life and honesty from John and am proud to say he was a true friend. I was angry with him when he was old for not having better medical treatment, particularly for his teeth. His only excuse to me was that he knew his illness was terminal and being a Scot, he was frugal! Perhaps, in hindsight, he had money problems. He never complained.

John was also a vibrant soul who knew how to let his hair down socially. I learned huge amounts from him as my friend. I often think of him.

Quite interesting that John and Geoff became friends through my family. I believe they both reciprocated my feelings for them; ie "I have got your back". I try to include this in my life for my friends and family. It's unadvertised protection.

(c) Ivor Johnson

The Big Fella! That's what another friend called him. Ivor was that in so many ways. A quiet, warm presence who only came into my life about 25 years ago.

The friendship began in a very low-key fashion. I had started an after-retirement, retail business in the beautiful small town of Woodend in the Macedon Ranges, north of Gisborne. A quiet small business selling aromatherapy products.

My wife Jay was in the shop one day and an imposing man walked up the street outside; I pointed him out to her, saying, "See that man, he has invited me into the local Rotary Club and the Traders Association." Over time, I joined both and got to know Ivor. A special benefit was that I gradually became a friend. We shared subtle attitudes that took time to be recognised.

Gradually, I learned about his humble background, his commercial and personal growth, and the complex family relationships involved, particularly in and around Woodend and the Macedon Ranges. In spite of the controversial nature of some historical events, long before my association, I never heard him say a personal bad word about any of those involved. In many ways their family events could be likened to the legendary American 'The Martins and The Coys' disputes.

Considerably younger than me, Ivor, it always seemed to me, had considered opinions on most things, and he personified calmness. We often chatted over wide-ranging issues and current topics of interest. He was a very generous-natured person.

The disputes within the families of Johnsons and Keatings would fill a book on their own, but credit to all those involved who retained their dignity. I was able to associate with most members of the families and am grateful for all the contacts.

Ivor to me was a 'gentle giant', with a wide, colourful and understated list of achievements. Apart from owning a substantial part of Woodend, he was a major influence in establishing and sustaining physically and financially the Woodend Rotary Club, the *Woodend Star* newpaper, the BoB's* lunch group and no doubt many other community events. Financial support for new groups and ideas were seldom publicly acknowledged. A free thinker with no ulterior motives; a true community supporter.

On a very personal scale, I have appreciation for how in his

---

* Bunch of Blokes. Informal social group with no formal agenda; a bit like a Men's Shed.

very low-key way, Ivor always included me. I sure as hell I do miss him!

Ivor and I were longstanding members of a 'boys only' club. Not quite a 'secret society' but members were selected by invitation only, where all were retired senior commercial executives. Referred to as the HC club—aka the Hunter Club. No agenda to raise funds or support causes. We met monthly, wore suits and had quality conversational lunches where we exchanged stories about ties and travels and current events. A bunch of old and 'like' souls. Years ago, we totalled around 30 members. Time, illness and passings gradually eroded the numbers until only four of us remained as close associates. The club was officially closed when the numbers slid down to under 10. A small number of us are continuing to meet. One of these is my close friend and fellow Rugby tragic Rob Owers. We are both ex Kiwis and huge supporters of the NZ All Blacks. Friends need things in common. A stark reminder of the fragility of life was recently ago when Rob fell down the stairs in his home and broke a leg in multiple places, and his ankle.

6

FAMILY

"We boil at different degrees." — Emerson

This is a section of my life that I have not handled with notable success.

I hasten to add my opinion that it has not necessarily been a total disaster, as I'm in close communications with my two children.

Not such a claim I can make about how it all goes with my grandchildren. I guess that's normal? My two sisters I can claim to be in 'courteous contact' with.

The propensity for broken marriages amongst my peers is not an excuse, and I had little or no idea, or gave any thought to the consequential ongoing negative effects on my two children of a divorce. The act of breaking my first marriage was probably the most selfish thing I have ever done. All these years later, I have never closely examined or had the opportunity to discuss the innermost effects my children harboured then or even now.

Does anyone ever have the 'complete relationship' with their children or even their own spouse? There is a huge question to be asked about that played by the traditional following of habits,

A Little Duck

With a bit of luck
A duck
Will come into your life

When you are at the peak
Of your great powers.
And your achievement towers
like a smoking chimney stack
There'll be a quack
And right there at your feet
A little duck will stand;
She will take you by the hand
And lead you
Like a child with no defence;
She will lead you
Into wisdom, joy and innocence.
That little duck.

We wish you luck.

Michael Leunig

beliefs, and behaviours of the older generation, or the habit of 'throwing out the baby with the bath water'. Human nature is so complex. When I flew the coop, it was a great act of selfishness. A combination of a desire for excitement, sexual exploration and pure single-minded irresponsibility.

Would others have been preparing mentally to do the same in due course? Can relationships ever be repaired? I will never know. However, I am very happy that my children have the mother they have.

I have observed with interest in recent years how my family and friends have aged.

Generalisations apply.

My older sister Margaret married into wealth. Not without a wide range of criticisms from within the family concerned, but a survivor she has been. Now ruling her own farm fiefdom. We all grow older and frailer, internally and externally. Some with warmth, generosity and acceptance, and some in other ways.

A general comment is that we sometimes quickly see fault in many young people and also in the old and frail. There are pathetic and selfish examples everywhere. There is always sad wastage in relationships that should and could have grown, blossomed and flourished. Families in particular.

A famous saying is, "Every family is unique in its own dysfunctionality."

Tolstoy said, "All happy families are alike, but every unhappy family is different."

What family traits are really inherited? I do not accept a description of being 'self-absorbed' or 'preoccupied'.

My younger sister Barbara fills me with joy. She is now a widow, who married young to an unlikely-to-succeed partner. It was a seriously bumpy ride but they stuck together for better or worse and she is now really enjoying some of the fruits of her labour and sacrifices.

My Father

In hindsight I wish my dad had supervised me on a more personal scale; been more obviously interested in 'seeing' what I was doing or achieving. You don't really know until later, when you do know, how solid and peaceful your good early home life was and the ongoing effect. My father Reg was quite undemonstrative, but never angry or cruel. Even now I miss the quality of extreme calm and thoughtfulness he provided.

He taught me to drive his car from about the time I could reach the pedals, i.e. from about 13 years of age, which enabled me to pitch up on my 15th birthday to pass my driver's tests with a skill I then didn't even know I had achieved.

Again, with hindsight, my father Reg was an interesting man. I mean not only physically. He was always interested and curious 'to just look around the corner'—just to see what was there. His curiosity was never-ending and he read at least one book a week, driving the local librarian crazy with his book requests and my mother as the messenger and collector. His eating habits were regular, timely, and small. Regular serves of meat, green vegetables and minimum lettuce was his mantra! Bacon, eggs and toast with a cup of tea.

Reg was funny about rules. A better word to describe him would be sensible, as he could push the envelope on some things but never ever on ethics. In an old-fashioned way, he was intolerant of lawlessness and became angry with men who assaulted their partners.

My father was unhappy with a member of our family who finished up with a problem, but he moved on. He drank little or no alcohol, although I heard him occasionally (as a doctor) recommend to a patient over the telephone to have a nip of whisky or brandy until he arrived. Those were the days when your doctor made house visits, even on the weekend or after 6pm. Payments from patients were often in the form of fruit and vegetables or even small personal homemade gifts when cash was tight.

Always his very first telephone question to patients ringing with an ailment was, "Have your bowels moved in the last couple of days?" To my childish amusement, some patients were not even sure what that meant and some thought it was about 'dowels' (building pegs).

My smart-arse answer to myself then would be, 'I reckon they have, as I have been down the road to meet Jason and I'm sure they came with me.' Dad would not have seen that as funny.

My father never tried to sow into my psyche any ambitions he may have had for himself or even his personal wishes he had for me to pursue or succeed in any particular area. I am grateful for that. I recall with much love and fondness my parents. When my father became elderly, he was crippled with extensive arthritis but he never ever complained.

These memories have bubbled to the surface late in my life and I know for sure my own children will hold totally different memories of me.

My Mother

I always did appreciate my mother. It's probably not until I have become older and she has 'passed' that I now fully appreciated the influence she had on me in my childhood. Her quiet influence just accumulated on and on. I had a very peaceful childhood compared to others I know.

I can only vaguely remember her crying twice: once when she had her arm caught in the washing machine ringer, and on another occasion when I think Dad was giving her some seriously bad health news.

She was totally unflappable and ran our home with much demonstrable love and care. When I was off to boarding school—which my parents considered was giving me the best educational opportunity—she organised all my clothing (probably new) and personally labelled it all. When I returned on holidays and even when I lived at home as a young adult, all the washing and cleaning—even my filthy football gear—never seemed to be chore. Labours of love indeed.

It never occurred to me then that Mum and Dad probably had plans and aspirations of their own. I guess as with all young people, it seemed to me that my plans were all-important—to everyone. They always welcomed into my life any of my new friends with love and affection. I was not wise enough to appreciate or to understand how their lives continued on and they had aspirations of their own for the future.

My mother was the nerve centre that kept our family news and relationships alive even though a lot went right past me. As is normal, I was busy growing up and enjoying new relationships always with the support of my parents. Sunday lunches were an important social event with little or no appreciation of the logistics concerned. It really does seem now at my older age that it is possible to fully admire and appreciate the effort and application needed to keep all of that active and ongoing. What a steady, calm and unflappable household I grew up in.

A small regret I have is I that did not have the foresight and planning to arrange and enjoy at least one anniversary or birthday party for them together as they aged.

Memories are important and perhaps even more so as I have got older; in particular—regarding my mother—as to how much nicer it would be for her to be remembered by everyone as the active and stylish woman she was in her heyday. Entertaining all and sundry and just being herself. Not as a frail and lost little old lady, as the grandchildren and others no doubt remember her.

An interesting observation is that as close as I was to Mum and Dad and knowing they both wore dentures, I never ever saw them without teeth in. They were always immaculate.

My Dad was a physically frail man when he became very old, but he was mentally sharp to the very end. His arthritis was very bad but he never complained.

Age is not necessarily kind.

It's always when thinking about my immediate family that my consciousness wanders not only around my mind games but in a shallow way into the 'soul.' I am genuinely agnostic, but curious to see if there is more proof or evidence associated with religious arguments—but it would have to be without any fear or repercussions. I genuinely enjoy visiting and the beauty of magnificent and different churches and places of worship of all faiths. The history and tradition behind it all fascinates me.

Another interest in family as I age is wondering what or where my Mum and Dad considered to be their 'home'. Was it where they grew up with us the children as the entire family? Or was it when and where they lived when they were first married? Or later where they chose to retire? Or just wherever they lived in the different times on their journey? My mother I think was most happy back in Auckland, where she was close to her twin sister and school friends, but with my dad, I really don't know.

When I observe the arrogance and privilege that some professionals, and the very-rich, appoint to themselves, I shudder about the toxic nature of human beings. Happily, my parents were modest in many ways. Perhaps this has contributed to keeping me grounded as I age.

I read "The Evolution of a person's ambition over their lifetime":

To be a circus clown,
To be like dad,
To be a fireman,
To do something noble,

To get wealthy,
To make ends meet,
To get the old age pension.

An inclusion in my highly rated family members has to be:
(d) Mary Ella Gamble
(my Aunty Meg. Born 1900, died 1984).

Meg, of course, must be in the very top section of my past. She was my mother's twin sister, and lived in Auckland, where I attended boarding school in Mt Albert. From the time I was 13 years old she was the only approved person for a Sunday exit from the school "House" that I could visit. From that time on, with great harmony, it was as if I had an additional mother.

Meg never married and was the most interesting and genuine friend I ever had. She was always interested in my goings on and was never critical—just interested, and also happy to state an opinion on subjects when asked. She used to pass on some points and laugh, saying, "Nothing to do with me, you better ask your Mum or Dad—they pay the bills!"

She treated me with genuine love as a child and then an adult, as she did Ngaire, which was happily reciprocated.

Some of her magical moments are related in my first book, 'What's it all About' and she deserves to be further recognised in this memoir's musings. Meg was super special. My mother also missed her dearly. I didn't want any of them to pass, and I wish I could magically simply say "abracadabra" and bring them back for a renewal of my love.

The following to me sums it all up: "A friend forgives your defects, and if he is very fond of you, he doesn't see any."

With hindsight it is clear that Meg was a major part of my recognising that there are variations and meanings to the words "I love you" and to whom I could say them. A recognition of my own inhibitions too.

No doubt many of the attitudes that have accompanied me through life have been shaped by all of the above, and even my early reading of books I still own, such as 'Robin Hood', 'Tom Sawyer', 'The Boys King Arthur', several histories of Winston Churchill, and Richie McCaw, a famous All Black rugby player and leader. Personal honour and old-fashioned values were drummed into me!

As I grew older, it was more fun reading books poking fun at 'Aussies' and 'Kiwis' separately!

It is now very apparent that I am not half as amusing or interesting or thoughtful as I once thought I was. My Dad used to refer to the odd person he did not like as having the gift of the gab and occasionally I genuinely try to check on myself. He gave me many life-lesson experiences without conscious knowledge. He really was a modest person.

To my family I say, "Thanks for tolerating me!"

This is a great arena for personal reflections both up and down the scale and to admire the world today and how friends and family are managing their own lives.

Am I my own worst enemy? Or do we all need our own consultancy?

My hope is that my words, integrity, honesty, (and humour) bubble to the top on most occasions. My sisters and I remain, I believe, warm courteous friends without any great influence or angst. That is quite an achievement!

To my two children I say a huge big thanks for keeping me on their friendship list. I love them both unconditionally, unreservedly and uncomplicatedly.

I recently saw the movie *Armageddon Time*, starring Anne Hathaway, Anthony Hopkins and Jeremy Strong, and it gave me a bit of a jolt about my own past behaviour when they were young.

Deliberately written in capital letters I say to Dene and Lianne, and especially to Jay,

"THANK YOU FOR BEING WHAT YOU ARE AND TREATING ME SO WELL!"

7
PERSONAL DISLIKES AND HEROES

(a) Dislikes

I really detest people who take credit for other people's achievements. Stealing credit for themselves.

Another big dislike is those who are quick to ridicule others' behaviour. So judgemental! And, those who believe they have 'infallible' judgement. My fervent belief has always been, "as you sow; so shall you reap". Or "People in glass houses shouldn't throw stones".

Those with uncontrollable tempers I avoid. Same for those who are determined to 'pay back'. No need to get even. Move on!

Man's inhumanity to fellow man. But how to control this?

Levels of flattery, both sincere and insincere, make me squirm. The giver has a motive perhaps?

Simple unfairness. Dictatorships. In any walk of life. Lack of opportunities. Apartheid rule in South Africa made me sick to the stomach.

DECLARATION OF ONE PERSON

Here I am.
Alive on earth.
Me.

Conscious.
Unconscious.
Semi-conscious.

Knowing others.
Known to others.

Yet also unknown, unknowable and alone forever.

Soon I will not be here.

HURRAH!

'He who talks like a man who is unable to keep up with his thoughts, no matter how rapidly he speaks!' As modest as a violet! Beware of those who talk too much!

(b) My Heroes

Nelson Mandela
Having lived in South Africa for five years, the person I admire most is Nelson Mandela. I have read several of the books about him. Such a true hero.

Roger Federer
In the sporting arena a real champion. What a modest guy, and so generous to others.

Probably as talented as Roger, but almost 'ugly natured' in comparison, was John McEnroe, who matured into a highly respected expert in several fields. Good on him.

Genuine leaders are few and far between, and probably are most obvious to observe on the sporting fields, as their star only shines for shorter periods than politicians, or even in commerce, or the more serious activities. Some are only recognised after they pass, which is more the pity.

Queen Elizabeth
I must acknowledge the influence of the recently departed Queen Elizabeth 2. People all over the world will have deep in their psyche the internal question and answer, "Where were you when you learned of the Queen's passing"?

Not many people or events fill me with "Awe and Respect" but Queen Elizabeth did.

I am a monarchist, even though I think 'born to be King or Queen' is absurd. The proof of that is easy to illustrate by naming Andrew and Harry!

I would have been happy to have QE2 live for ever as an illustration of total service to the community. She was not necessarily an outstanding aggressive leader but she gave us her all regarding loving lifelong service. She earned our respect, unlike those who take positions of power by force. We hope they will be forgotten long after Queen Elizabeth is fondly remembered by people all over the world.

It will be interesting to see how King Charles moves into his new role, and be seen not as a silly 'tree-hugger' but as a serious environmentalist and deep thinker (which I think he clearly is); and as the new caretaker of vast riches, and of land that (perhaps) in part could be converted into meaningful uses for many more people, or to be able to revert into more village/community lifestyles enjoyed in so much of the world.

I am not sure who this quote is attributed to but for me it applied to Queen Elizabeth. When asked to explain the secret to living a long life she simply responded, "Don't die!"

I like the following quote too—perhaps QE2 was an end result of it too? "Half the work that is done in this world, is to make things appear what they are not." — E R Beable.

(c) Villains

All too often the 'WTF!' comment applies to the antisocial "idiots" of society. They have no thought of community values or even any decent respect for fellow human beings.

Recent human behaviour politically and internationally has risen to a height of causing (almost) global moral outrage, with the level of unsupported actions taken by Russia.

Australian ex-Prime Minister Morrison for also exceeding past performances. Democracy has taken care of that now, after the ex-PM secretly added five new areas of ministerial power.

Only time will tell if fair and decent behaviour will prevail in the global arena.

8
USEFUL ANY MORE?

"The man who listens to reason is lost; reason enslaves all whose minds are not strong enough to master her." — Shaw

Does this mean that humans should always retain a sense of fun?
    Another poem of significance that has been with me throughout my life is the poem *The Soldier* by Rupert Brooke.

> "If I should die, think only this of me:
> That there's some corner of a foreign field
> That is for ever England. There shall be
> In that that rich earth a richer dust concealed;
> A dust whom England bore, shaped, made aware,
> Gave once, her flowers to love, her ways to roam,
> A body of England's, breathing English air
> Washed by rivers, blest by suns of home.
>
> And think, this heart, all evil shed away,
> A pulse in the eternal mind, no less
> Gives somewhere back the thoughts by England given;
> Her sights and sounds; dreams as happy as her day;
> And laughter, learnt of friends; and gentleness,
> In hearts at peace, under an English heaven."

You can fool some of the people all of the time...

...and you can fool all of the people some of the time.

But you only need to fool a majority of the people for one day every few years..

...and you've got a democracy!

Leunig

I wonder,
Will it all click into place?
I feel it might.
I had a glimpse
That things could all
Come right.

I'd wake up
On a sunny, slightly roostered morn.
And wouldn't realise at first;
The rightness would take time
To dawn.

And gradually
The thing would start to gleam,
This worried life I'd had;
This awful world;
This painful mess;
It was, in fact,
A kind of dream!

The penny would just drop
Into my hand —
The penny that I'd lost
So long ago —
And all the peace
Withheld and blocked from me
Would start to flow.

The gentle hum;
The gold and silver light
Would all resume:
The fairies and the pixies,
The particles of dust
Caught in the sunlight
In my room.

I'd pick up
Where I had been so rudely
Interrupted
I'd have it back again for keeps:
My dog, my brilliant grasp of life,
My back yard and my paddocks
full of time
The world all glad around me
My rightful place —
My joyous leaps.

Leunig

This poem was written in 1914. It is a deeply patriotic and idealistic poem in the first year of the first world war. Now the poem is regarded as perhaps naïve, but it captures feelings of loyalty and trust. Modern wars seem to be bereft of such great pride. In a strange parallel way, I identify with much of it.

How important is personal experience, and human bigotry to those growing up? When does maturity finally click in and provide a better balance in assessing risks, forming opinions, that in turn may graduate to more valuable judgements and contributions to own families and society? Is the result more infallible and better?

The thing I find interesting is the easy way my mind can rationalise or even appease for my sometimes extraordinary or absurd opinions. I can make my own personal (internal) judgements with no problems on every and any subject without a care. I can rationalise, expand, or minimise, as the day goes on. My drive to reach a conclusion is energetic but often is basically founded on, "What is the truth? Is it my truth only?"

One of the wonders of older age is to be able to pickpocket ideas from completely different arenas. What can possibly be wrong with that?

My mind has everything covered. It doesn't have to go anywhere, or show anything, and I attain 'peace of mind' and contentment. I do, however, still have some inhibitions in many areas regarding public display of my body.

In a strange way, small leaderships taken from the time I was young, should have contributed to a lonelier life than that I have enjoyed. It is commonly agreed that in becoming a leader (of any type) you forfeit some of the rights to be one of the crowd. You are expected to leave functions early enough to allow others time to enjoy. You must put up with people telling you (instructing you) with things you already know. You must show patience and tolerance to all, and handle 'nonsense' with style and grace. Most of all distribute praise where it is due, without expecting reciprocal response. Be seen to be fair, but consistently firm.

More than one lifetime is needed to absorb and implement such high ideals. From being a part of or even captain of a sporting team whilst young, through being a school prefect, and obtaining commercial leadership successes, one's character and personality is developed and expanded.

To what I am today, an older and, hopefully, wiser man!

The big question for everyone is, "How much time do I have left?" What can I achieve with what is left? Does it matter?

One more poem (before I desist from the use), as the last two lines printed in Verse 3 are now important.

Break, Break, Break
By Alfred Lord Tennyson

"*Break, break, break.*
On thy cold grey stones, O Sea!
And I would that my tongue could utter
The thoughts that arise in me.

O, well for the fisherman's boy,
That he shouts with his sister at play!
O, well for the sailor lad,
That he sings in his boat on the bay!
And the stately ships go on
To their haven under the hill;
But O for the touch of a vanished hand,
And the sound of a voice that is still!

Break, break, break
At the foot of thy crags, O Sea!
But the tender grace of a day that is dead
Will never come back to me".

Where does the old world of collectors (of memories, products, antiques and just 'things') fit now that they (the things) are aged? Do they need identification and 'proof' of original creation or ownership, to make them more emotionally valuable? Just because they are old do they have a value? Lots of old things have no value at all.

A close friend is a collector of worldwide tennis memorabilia, and he is 100% completely sane. He attends all the high-level sporting events, and in fact was rebuked by a leading sporting female when he asked—in his best and most polite manner— would she sign a programme. She very impolitely told him, "F--- off!" Classy!!! It didn't faze him one bit. My point is that anything that brings joy from the mere fact of collecting is a plus.

I think collecting stamps as a hobby probably sounds a bit

more of a soft and sound reason 'to be'. It is today a much-diminished hobby, as fewer and fewer letters are now posted.

I often wonder to myself what is out there in the future for the world? Is an Armageddon likely? Is an atomic holocaust likely to evolve, or can we trust world leaders to avoid such a catastrophe?

I think I am a lightweight in many areas. The Cuban Missile Crisis never cut through my concern for world peace years ago, but today the current Russia v Ukraine war crisis is of great interest, and I think has elements for others to duplicate in both good and bad ways. Hopefully, modern communications and visual coverage may discourage catastrophe.

I often wonder if I am my own best friend, or my own worst enemy? That requires some imagination. Perhaps I will ask those closest to me.

I now have a high level of contentment that has gradually sneaked up on me.

9
GENERAL THOUGHTS ON LIFE AND LOVE

"One must be a god to be able to tell successes from failures without making a mistake." — Chekhov

I am very comfortable within my own skin. Figuratively and literally.

As a young child, I was a bedwetter later than I should have been, but my parents tolerated that without any blame game, and my attacks of asthma seemed to disappear around the age of 12. No angst passed over to me. Physically, for the rest of my life, it never troubled me to be seen growing up in New Zealand, as a "skinny little white boy" and as an adult to be still seen as a lanky adult.

My achievements in my sports of choice have been adequate and probably cushioned me. My parents also no doubt sheltered me from some of the unpleasant reactions other kids endured. Sports have always been a useful introduction to many levels of social interaction for me ongoing, even as an adult.

It is accurate to admit I have been extremely lucky in love and life. Early in adulthood, I was in love with a very special person, whom I married and we produced two children. Through my

then bad judgement and later bad behaviour, I was to blame for the breakdown of that relationship and marriage.

A new and very different relationship evolved and is still very much intact today. Acknowledgement at the highest level must be included in this memoir to it.

Sport has always served me well, both as social introductions as a player and because I have a wide breadth and depth of interest in most sports. Tennis has opened contacts and friendships in many different places and countries. As I age, I still have the basics to be competitive with ground strokes but the mechanics of throwing the ball up to serve seem to be deserting me more often!

Perhaps I'll have a go at bowls.

Now for the first time some body functions are underperforming and have to be coped with. Luckily modern medicine is counteracting or controlling these current weaknesses.

My inhibitions are much lower but I'm seldom tempted to carry out the absurd. Peeing in a public toilet is still no problem nor should it ever be, having enjoyed boarding school and its ways.

I was a hopeless dancer in my school days, and my mother tried to help with arranging some lessons at home in the holidays. I can still recall the name of a Joan Ritchie who made valiant efforts to teach me to waltz and quick step. I was hopeless, and sadly am not much better today. Clumsy. Shortcomings of not able to hear or catch the rhythm. This is surprising when other areas of coordination are good. And with a few drinks, I go ok at rock and roll!

As a young child I was teased for having big ears. "Aeroplane ears, glider wings" I was called and the like. No doubt this added to my shyness and reticence to step forward full of confidence. I often wonder how different my personality might have been had two simple operations on my prominent ears been carried out, as they would be today?

I now am in a position to be able to consider the enjoyment of luxuries. The word 'more' is seldom in my vocabulary, except in relation to there being more education for all and the better protection of the environment.

Recent experiences never seem so very notable. Travel experiences are enjoyed. But real 'triumphs' do not exist, because mature socialising keeps things always in proportion. Constant joy and happiness are always there but are often realised in past tense whilst reflecting, even if only on a day or two ago. There are no current issues to concern me really.

The word 'consequences' and all its full meaning, is quite low on my internal horizon. There is no concern about inappropriate or even appropriate curiosity/behaviour. There is not much today that I am likely to be locked up over.

Decision making still gives me satisfaction and although I make decisions more slowly, I am better as I share more. Or is that compulsory now in today's new world?

I have a word I can and do use in a variety of circumstances. The word is 'interesting'. I use it mostly when I am bored shitless or I don't fully understand the subject someone is perhaps rabbiting on about. Sometimes it is about the real divide between city and country attitudes, or perhaps even on the subject of

THE PLODDER.

You'll get left behind!

HOW WONDERFUL.

You'll miss out!

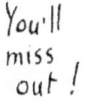

HOW LOVELY.

You won't be Influential!

HOW TRUE.

You won't achieve your personal best!

HOW ENJOYABLE.

You won't be attractive!
You won't be clever!

HOW DIVINE.

You won't know what's happening!

HOW PEACEFUL.

etc.

Leunig

personal tattoos! Body Art? It can be about perceived toughness or even 'manhood'.

I think it is not being dishonest but more a way of letting many subjects go through to the keeper. It also allows me to hide my bias and perhaps some bigotry. Don't talk about it, let it go through. Letting others have their say?

I believe I am allowed to still speculate in my mind about whether or not the little gnomes tapping away in my basement being productive really exist!

10
COMMERCE AND LIFE TODAY

"A wise man knows everything; a shrewd one also knows everybody!" — Anonymous

This is the easy chapter. It's a bit similar to life. I call it shadow boxing. You can throw all the punches and never get hurt. Most of the action is in my mind. I'm now here only as an observer and carry no commercial responsibilities. There is not much that I can't rationalise when I'm wrong, and little or no harm when I stuff up. I can practise and desire all things in my mind and in my soul.

IT expertise is not one of my great skills so I probably have been lucky to sneak by at the end of my full commercial experience by still having enough help to get by. Executives today must keep their own diaries, send and answer a high proportion of their emails and correspondence, so they are often overstressed. There are no time limits on working time vs time off.

Computer screens full of complex diagrams, formulae and equations that require instant evaluation and instant answers,

On the armchair, a book: "HOW TO RELAX"

Beside the bed, a book; "HOW TO GET TO SLEEP"

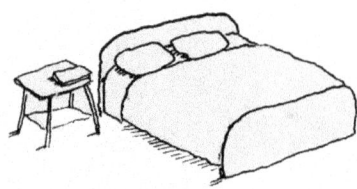

Next to the man, a book; "HOW TO BE A MAN"

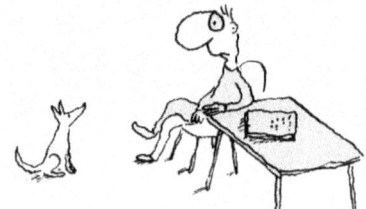

Next to the window, a book; "HOW TO SEE WHAT'S IN FRONT OF YOU"

On the desk, a book: HOW TO SUCCEED IN LIFE"

In hell, a book; "HOW YOU ENDED UP IN HELL"

which suggests room for errors. Make "more haste less speed" as one of my tutors used to say.

My current level of infallible judgement is not put to any real tests because I can in my mind simply move anything onto other matters, or even other opinions I have heard. The elaborate use of acronyms in many areas of life is no longer a challenge because my reputation, my need to understand what is going on, is not at risk. At my current age, I can get by with asking for a definition. The ego no longer exists. Perhaps the word 'mellowing' must enter my vocabulary.

I wake up most mornings 'fresh as a daisy' because I don't have to care and have no worries.

The word integrity keeps bouncing to the top of my mind and in many ways that is reassuring. Many of the old adages that were genuinely second nature in business are standing me well in retirement; 'responsibility must be accompanied with authority'. Also, 'You can't be either half in or half out'.

You must be able to trust friends. They are not limited partners. Not quite the same as business where it worked well to always 'be friendly, but not friends.'

Commerce was an area which helped me to establish who were my true friends. I am lucky to claim perhaps four from commerce, two from secondary school days who are still alive, and six from more-recent history. These are really true friends I can trust with my innermost feelings and rely on their integrity to honour my deepest thoughts and rescue me without hesitation when needed. They are few indeed.

It is acceptable to occasionally 'dance with the enemy' in the mind, and can be stimulating to consider why they are what they are, and for what reason, without getting burnt.

At my age, there are fewer and fewer opportunities to practise integrity. It is, however, reassuring that just as in 'muscle memory' my brain or mind seems to act in the well-practised manner. Sad really, though, that my radical thinking is less, and when and how to use it, a small problem.

It must be frustrating for 'good' politicians that an inability to convince a working majority to consider or enact even mildly radical actions happens. Changing existing systems to be better is hard enough, let alone radically changing a system or completely throwing it out. The consequences add up to make it all very hard.

"Time and patience," said Tolstoy!

Sitting on the sidelines, current commerce is easy to assess. Why decisions are made; the politics, democracy, and even international consequences. All needing immediate responses. So much has changed though. For me now, expertise in modern communications immediately sets me behind the eight ball. I am slow and inaccurate as a typist and in most things IT. I find all modern forms of communications wonderful and my own inadequacies frustrating. I know some of it is pure laziness to put in the practice to learn and I blame the fact that all my senior commercial life I had excellent secretarial support. However, we didn't burn out so easily and so often then.

My thoughts on the current workplace and new jobs: I often pass the opinion that today, I would hate to be in the market for new employment. So much rapid technological change. It seems the skill level bar is now set so high, plus the embracing of current community opinions and the needs of all and sundry, would put many jobs in the too hard basket for me. The issue of being lonely as the boss is often heard. My best mentor's advice from 50 years ago still resonates with me, 'Be friendly but not friends'.

How does that all relate to achieving a promotion or a new job? It usually requires the confidence to try for new skills and new experiences. A stretch of abilities, new and good for the ego, the stimulation and confidence to think you can succeed. It is hoped and anticipated you will have enough 'smarts' to push through using the authority and power needed to lead the new team to success; an awareness of connections and relationships that are needed to succeed.

In general terms, in a new role, it is common for no one to know you and a proportion of the new associates perhaps want you to fail. Hard-won qualifications and expertise, experience and hard work should get you through. Have you got it in you? Are you aware of the sacrifices? Be aware of those who inflate their own skills to remain significant, when there is a more sensible utilisation to fill the need.

When deep in thought about this subject I recall probably my best mentor (and my first Managing Director) used the term "dirty pool". Simply, it meant the rules could be slightly bent but ultimately you would not benefit if it wasn't what was deemed 'normal decent practice'.

It is interesting to me that I don't miss wearing business suits, travelling business or first-class, or attending the canape and fluted champagne events. Or having appointments that seem important, or having to travel through customs and airports to many parts of this colourful and interesting world. No regrets!

However, it's also a good time to remember why I changed jobs in the past. The honest response is ambition, frustration, money, and to be happy with family culture and environment.

I have time for ruminating and no doubt time for modification of old opinions.

One of my closest female friends from many years ago warned me, "All work and no play makes Jack a dull boy!"

11
EMPLOYMENT

S to S — the Shell Company to Specsavers Ltd;
with a little sport mixed in between

How fortunate to be selected by Shell straight from school. That meant formal quality commercial training, and time allocated to my university studies. How lucky to be absorbed into what is now the old fashioned 'family' culture that existed in good companies in those days. 1953. Even luckier with connections, that one of the executives had a senior position in the Grammar Football Club and he eased my way through selections. I got to play a game or two on Eden Park.

My rejection of the overseas opportunity in Holland with the Shell HO Group for greater things within the company was treated then with compassion by them. I learned a lot, which probably taught me many things both commercially and personally in later life.

Employment in South Africa as Managing Director of an international company came with the responsibility that I had an effect on over 400 employees and their families. It would be irresponsible not to be aware of that.

My last significant commercial role was as a Director and Consultant for Specsavers Ltd Australia. My various roles were always directly to the Founder/Managing Director Doug Perkins, and working with members of the senior executive team.

Suffice to say Doug Perkins could and should be used as an example as to how a large diverse and dynamic international company can be run. The fact that he was always available for communications and had the ability to succinctly arrive at the correct conclusion, and deliver most answers in a relaxed fashion, made him special.

It helped that he played many sports well, including rugby. The Welsh and NZ have a history!

The part of the mind that once held poems is now used for storing passwords.

The part of the mind that once remembered songs is now used for storing PIN numbers

The part of the mind that once helped us to hold each other is how used for processing media content.

The part of the mind that once had no apparent function: it's still as mysterious as ever. It's our greatest hope.

Work days are now well behind me, with little or no regrets. I have resisted the collection of plaques or framed wall prints signifying 'how great I am (or was?)'.

My bucket list does include areas in which I had hopes.

What is a real achievement, and who is the judge? It doesn't matter! Now I can be an expert on everything. Being lucky to have survived into a form of longevity it is no longer a surprise that events of significance are over in a short period of time.

How best to urge friends and family to enjoy life as it goes along? My contemplations within the mind are often joined by ruminations about whether there is room for a soul.

Today my own past personal workplace indiscretion (with Jay) would probably be deemed inappropriate in the business world.

Modern Technology

Now we are into a subject I do not know well at all. I just get by. But to participate in modern everyday life, I must handle the basics.

A friend (in my age group) related this week that he had just purchased a brand-new luxury sedan and when he explained why he bought such a highly technological machine he offered, "I bought it only because I liked the look of it", i.e., not for all the whizz bang IT in it, which I may never use!" Maybe absurd in this day and age?

The fear of not being able to cope with the advances being made in every sphere are real but not paramount. I have a mobile phone that like most of us, I rely on to converse and to keep in touch with all and sundry. It has hundreds of apps that I do not use, and do not want to use, but I do have to sometimes ask for help and direction. I have an iPad that in some miraculous way (!) is connected to my mobile phone and other devices, which is useful to contact Google for information, and to watch some more remote sports streaming on it.

I also have this wonderful laptop that has allowed me to play at being an author. None of these magic machines would be worth 'a penny-worth of salt' without the constant on-call help and advice from the constant technological magician, my wonderful, very patient wife and also best friend, Jay.

I can handle a stapling machine, some basic texts, and make a telephone call on my mobile and use 'WhatsApp'. Fax machines are now so far behind in my 'action days'—does anyone remember them? Remember toll calls?

I am full of wonderment about the Bonningtons who arrived in New Zealand in 1849 (in my Book 1) and who sent an immediate letter back to family in the UK 'to get to NZ as quickly as possible'. The communication and actions took about a year to complete. Today, we frequently fly between Cairns and Melbourne and back, sometimes just to, say, attend a funeral or to be able to come and go to catch up with friends and neighbours within very short time frames.

When I first commenced work, a fax machine and a Burroughs accounting monster were the major commercial innovations.

I don't know anyone who now owns or uses one, or repairs such a machine. Modern technology today is simply amazing.

"Success is not final, failure is not fatal. It is the courage to continue that counts". —Winston Churchill

12.

LONELINESS

"Know thyself. If I knew myself, I'd run away." — Goethe

To me, the secret of old age is an ability to ignore any thoughts of loneliness. My personal mantra now, aged over 88, is to try to never be grumpy, to stay happy and positive—even though time inevitably keeps moving on.

Look in a mirror and that tells that everything, including family and friends, are eroding. Don't be cantankerous, as it is really ugly. The plans of mice and men are little more than Karma in the bigger scheme of things.

Over many years I have tried to examine and consider my own psyche; tried to evaluate both my own conscious and unconscious minds.

Loneliness can be nothing more than a state of mind, or simply a craving for some human company with others, and not even those people in the category who 'behave like me.'

In a tiny way, I do miss what the word 'intimate' means, and its fuller mental meaning that requires a profound depth of trust with friends. I really miss my very close deceased friends. I have discovered that loneliness and isolation go together but

positivity about why we are here and what we can contribute, gets me through.

Some people wish they could be like birds that can up and fly away, while others may enjoy visiting zoos or a wildlife sanctuary (like those in South Africa) that just fill their minds with wonderment. Space travel is a completely separate subject.

Our minds and spirits can fluctuate all over the place.

The secret I have discovered is to live comfortably within the current parameters. Keep it all in a clear mind and try to keep it all simple. We all grow old and frail inside and outside our minds. Sometimes the judgement is that it is always the young who are troubled and the old who are pathetic. I don't hold that opinion, but I have witnessed traits that are extreme, permanent and contribute to negative results and denials.

I do admit I often wonder to myself, regarding many different spheres, "Why me, or Why not me?"

Health and Happiness

Well, it is a triumph to be alive. There is no secret formula for this. Some young people are absolute boofheads and some old people are magnificent. And vice versa! We have all shades in between.

Jay and I have travelled widely and have enjoyed wonderful experiences together.

My favourite poem about travel is *Ozymandias* by PB Shelley (1792-1822). It is ageless.

Ozymandias

"I met a traveller from an antique land
Who said: "Two vast and trunkless legs of stone
Stand in the desert—Near them, on the sand
Half sunk, a shattered visage lies,
Whose frown,
And wrinkled lip, and sneer of cold command,
Tell that its sculptor well those passions read
Which yet survive, stamped on these lifeless things,
The hand that mocked them and the heart that fed;
And on the pedestal, these words appear:
My name is Ozymandias, King of Kings;
Look on my Works, ye Mighty, and despair!
Nothing beside remains. Round the decay
Of that colossal Wreck, boundless and bare
The lone and level sands stretch far away".

For me this poem keeps most things in perspective. Egypt is full of wonders and the talent that was so advanced so long ago. The poem reinforces that nothing lasts forever!

Health, wealth, and happiness are important, but I think body and soul are more important. The act of dying is never far away for anyone, and terminal illness certainly adds to the personal focus.

Should this knowledge now change behaviour, does time become more precious, and what side effects arise from the prognosis? It would be good to know the actual change-over date!

An "Energy Pill" would be a physical plus. I am not sure that would work as well for the brain, but most people have a need for physical stimulation. More and more, I relate to the brain and the soul as I age. Both mystify me as I wrestle with so-called high intelligence (over-rated?), anxiety, family relationships, and performance under or over expectations when under pressure. It's nearly all in the brain and many experts consider brain training helps. Is that energy?

Where does fear fit? Of the known and or the unknown. Is it a result of personal or non-personal experience? Or just the imagination of the brain? The mind can be so reassuring.

I have wondered for years what is success, and who makes that judgement? Are we individually happy by our own judgement? Is that enough?

When wanting to be 'good'—how can one reach out? A good example of this predicament occurred recently when I was in a 'quiet carriage' on the train from Melbourne to Gisborne. A young couple got on at Footscray station—probably going on up to Bendigo. They were young, well dressed, good looking. They crouched together holding hands and hugging in the warmest possible way. The woman had a steady flow of tears and regular breaks off to the toilet. They were obviously saddened and distressed by an event in their joint lives.

I considered their situation for the 50 minutes of my trip and by observation. My quandary was whether to volunteer any input out of kindness. I did not, although in happy and open situations I believe I have an ability to contribute worthwhile suggestions. I still wonder today what it was all about. More and more I believe an intrusion into their world today would not have been welcomed. More is the pity.

Dreams have appeared over my horizons and I am finding them interesting. Different ones it seems are now evolving, probably relative to my current medical treatment. The demons that come vividly onto the screen of my mind can be repetitious but occasionally weird. They vary, often in tune with natural or chemically induced sleep, and if early or late in the evening. I often feel as if I am winning against a downward spiral, and have episodes of defiance, anger and despair in short bursts. Only rarely do I want to share the content, as I understand I am only dreaming and the dark passageways of the mind are lifted as light emerges with dawn. Common sense seems to assert itself! The supernatural is not in my vocabulary.

The non-dreaming side of my personality jumps to the fore when I go for my long and dawdling walks around the neighbourhood, always in daylight. I could well be taken for an old lost person as I stop and look at all sorts of things that others perhaps do not see. I comment to myself about the beauty of gardens, cats, dogs, walls, fences, cars, garages, trees, clouds, the smell of freshness and the lack of noise. I observe cars and buildings. No wonder a walk takes me time. Always curious!

There has to be a section on Luck

Everyone rabbits on about there being no such thing. It is all a result of the hard work and dedication that the 'lucky ones' have put in. That is no doubt partially true but there is also a lot of 'BS' in such a trite and glib contribution. I believe it's a combination of things.

For example, the Covid-19 virus pandemic has illustrated the luck factor regarding the catching of it, treatment of it, and levels of death that resulted in different places because of it. We are really so lucky to be in Australia in spite of the variances we get in different states, and the levels of 'democracy', relative to the virus and the vaccines available. I am aware that many people have been seriously unwell but that is more than just the luck of the draw.

Similarly, my prostate cancer after many years in containment quite suddenly being reinvigorated has been 'Karma'. Modern medicine is a marvel. Living with the side effects of ill health in general terms is better than the alternative.

My honesty to openly admit to any health failings has always been constrained. My natural reserve means not admitting to friends and relations my health situation. I am so lucky that modern medicine is so wonderful. Also, luckily for me alcohol has never been a big part of my life.

> I like this joke for many reasons!
> "Does your husband talk in his sleep?"
> "No, and it is terribly exasperating. He just grins."

My dreams are full on, as are my days. I am never bored. I can almost conjure up my most favourite dream and can certainly get a continuance after I need a toilet break in the night that only half wakes me. My not so favourite dream is one in which I am lost, or the more recurring one in which I am chased by a bull. Never hurt though!

I am intrigued to watch some people with dogs who go to great lengths to avoid the responsibility of cleaning up the 'do-do' left by their dog in a public arena. Do they avoid responsibilities in other arenas?

"Since we cannot get what we like, let us like what we can get"
— Spanish proverb.

13

ILL HEALTH

"Life is not a spectacle or a feast; it is a predicament." — Santayana

A hard one to deal with. I reiterate: modern medicine is marvellous.

Aren't I so lucky to have this wonderful benefit of extension of life; perhaps there are others in my circle of friends or family receiving it as well?

Easy and trite to summarise with, 'That's Life'. For those with a genuine faith in their religion that provides an after-death assurance, it can no doubt help the inevitable.

Modern medical remedies eliminate many of the old early killers, and palliative treatment prolongs the inevitable and makes it more comfortable. In this circumstance what leaps to mind is 'graciousness'. Not bitterness.

The Queen had natural grace and I wonder if the world would be a much better place if we all had a little more of it.

The continuous deterioration of physical faculties is noticeable and can be depressing, but in my case, having passed the proverbial 'three score and ten', I say to myself, "just be grateful for small mercies." Though that was much easier said

The rose bush —
an arch conservative
with cruel thorns.

DEATH — the right-
wing radical.

The heartless, dull
bureaucracy of time.

The cat?
The cat is probably
a monarchist!

The dog — a naked
opportunist; a moral
vacuum; an uneducated,
pleasure-driven philistine.

And the moon —
so aloof, so cold
so full of itself.

Leunig.

than done when I was informed of my current prognosis.

Happily, for me the side effects of medication, such as mood changes, depression, headaches, and hot flushes do seem to be limited. Best to ask Jay how well I have coped!

The actual cost of my medication is astronomical, but I am lucky enough to fit into a category of huge government public list medical subsidies that makes it all possible. I am extremely grateful to be given the chance. The ongoing natural decay of physical and mental faculties is unrelenting and thus experimentation must be worth a go. Deterioration of my ability to play tennis at a reasonable level so far is not notably obvious (except to me!), and I have always preached the principle in life, 'Keep It Simple, Stupid'.

That is my wisdom for today. I am sure many in my current position would be full of optimism and not wanting to discuss it with all and sundry.

Progression of age and health

It is hard not to be aware of declining faculties because I don't want to know or observe them very well, and I am apparently even resisting acknowledgment of my apparent declining hearing. That makes Jay a little bit grumpy some days.

For years I treated my health problems with a high degree of secrecy, even from close friends and family. I'm not sure today of the reasoning but maybe I always relied on 'The Bell of Hope' syndrome, foolish as that now all seems. The serious upward movement in my PSA test for prostate cancer shocked that thinking along. The height of optimism!

The realities of ongoing life slip away from my mind as, like most of us, age and the progressions that accompany everyday living are not always noted. I do see changes in friends and relatives, particularly when I have not seen them for a month or two.

Maybe the same applies in reverse. But no one ever voices, "You look terrible." It seems to have some sort of connection not to pass a real opinion on the past or the future.

It might be a good idea to establish a 'Health Vane' for individuals, to be like a weather vane that we can carry in our pockets for showing to genuine inquiries to see how the wind is blowing in our own little atmosphere. The traditional hello and greeting, "How are you" can wear a little thin, and I always get a smile from my regular GP when he greets me, by my smart-arse reply to him: "I have no idea, can't you tell me?"

Most of the time, until I am seriously mentally or physically crippled, (and if the 'damage' is invisible) I prefer to just refer to 'ongoing maintenance'—illustrated, if need be, with arrows pointing up, down or sideways.

People do occasionally ask me "what do you attribute your health, longevity and happiness to?" Not quite in order of importance I suggest in my case it has been:

Parentage in a secure home.

Liking exercise.

Early morning starts.

Laughter. The ability to laugh at myself more than at others. I like humour.

Going to sit by the sea, the river or lake and watch the gulls or sparrows and feed them a little. Reflection.
Deep breathing to cope with stress.
Being a 'big kid' at heart. Not taking myself very seriously.
Always looking forward with optimism.

"He who has health, has hope; and he who has hope, has everything." — Arab proverb.

I used to have an attitude or arrogance (unsaid) that was; 'Toughen up, Princess! Only the weak get sick' and the like…

Maybe that has come back to bite me.

I have always been a keen runner or jogger so I think I can steal from a very old document praising/joking about the value of walking:

Walking can add minutes to your life.
This enables you at 85 years old
To spend an additional five months in a nursing home

I like long walks,
Especially when they are taken
By people who annoy me.

I have to walk early in the morning,
Before my brain figures out what I am doing!

We all get heavier as we get older,
Because there's a lot more information in our heads.
That's my story and I'm sticking to it.

14
MUSIC

"Music is well said to be the speech of angels." — Thomas Carlyle

Perhaps alcohol would have helped me to a more relaxed and earlier enjoyment of music!

> 'Rock and Roll; I Gave you the Best Years
> of My Life' By Kevin Johnson
>
> I can still remember when I bought my first guitar
> Remember just how good the feeling was,
> put it proudly in my car
> And my family listened fifty times to my two-song repertoire
> I told my mom her only son was going to be a star...
>
> Well, I bought all the Beatles records, sounded just like Paul
> Bought all the old Chuck Berrys, 78s and all
> And I sat by my record player playing every note they played
> I watched them all on TV, copied every move they made
>
> Oh, Rock'n'Roll I gave you all the best years of my life
> All the dreamy sunny Sundays, all the moon-lit summer nights

Summer diary

Yesterday I read the newspaper.

It sucked the life out of me

A feeling of gloomy bitterness and futility dragged me to the floor.

The dog came and began to lick my face

After about five minutes of licking, hope started to return to my body;

... not much, but enough for me to be able to slowly sit up and say, "good dog"

Leunig

*I was so busy in the back room, making love songs to you
But you were changin' your direction and I never even knew
That I was always, just one step behind you...*

Several more verses about 'time' such as sixty-six and seventy-one, and the frustration of trying to be a star, but always 'one step' behind the star time. A lovely tribute to life and persistence that does not guarantee success.

Another success by Kevin Johnson, 'She's Leaving (Bonnie please don't go) was close enough to be enjoyed. Both my sister and I were called Bonnie on occasions as kids.

*"She's leavin'
She's leavin'
She's on the ship now and leavin'
Standing by the gangway tossing streamers over her way
I find it kinda hard believin'
Deceivin'
Deceivin'
My subtle game of Deceivin'
Standing here and waving, blowing kisses and behaving
Like it doesn't matter much to see her leavin'*
Chorus
*I don't know what I don't know who
I don't know where she's going to
I only know she's going out of my life
Across the sea of waving hands and Colonel Billie's farewell band
I watch the disappearing face of my wife
And I'm doing all I can to hide the sad confusion of my mind
And to brace myself with every trick I know*

> *But though my lips are beating time*
> *To the words of Auld Lang Syne*
> *My voice keeps on defying*
> *Crying Bonnie please don't go."*
>
> Chorus.

And other lyrics were added by others.

I still listen to an eclectic range of music, mainly popular ballads, by popular vocalists. Not quite like a child being cuddled into relaxed sleep, but I often fall asleep at night in bed listening to music of my choice.

Some favourites include Judy Collins *Someday Soon*, Linda Ronstadt *Blue Bayou*, America *A Horse With No Name*, Leonard Cohen *Hallelujah*, *Suzanne* and several of his other renditions.

Another of significance to me is Johnny Cash, in his *Man in Black*—the final line says words to the effect that until racial and other bigotry has disappeared, he will continue to wear black. We have a long way to go.

15
BEMUSED AND APPALLED

"The malicious have a dark happiness." — Victor Hugo

There are everyday happenings that fall under this heading.

The long overdue return of the Murugappan family to Biloela in Queensland is a classic example of government being bogged down by rules and controls far overriding common sense and decency. Now with great common sense the remedy has been applied.

If anyone is ridiculous enough to suggest a stampede will follow, I say 'get real'. The country desperately needs new immigrants. A mistake or two will not start WW3 or 4.

The absurd scale and loss of life in the Russian invasion of Ukraine illustrates the absurdity of old men, old tribalism, old grudges, and an old reluctance to challenge misused power.

I dislike even having to include the name of Putin in my little memoir but clearly the fact that one man is putting at risk the entire future of our world is ridiculous. The killing of innocent people including children, the frail and defenceless is terrible. It is the work of a psychopathic serial killer. There have been

plenty before in history and they have been widely condemned. How long can functioning democracies hold up their heads and even agree to meet and shake the hand of such a criminal. It is insanity! And this in 2023!

Churchill famously said, "Russia is a riddle, wrapped in a mystery, inside an enigma."

I can only comment that the Ukraine invasion is like 'boofhead' or even mad behaviour, and with people like that the least you can do is seriously isolate them and take away any powerbase they think they have.

Man's inhumanity to man is on record everywhere but surely there is learning all around us. Look at climate change, and good steps towards cooperation to save the world.

Events of this magnitude can never be dropped into the basket of 'WTF!' items that gather exclamations but not much serious cooperative reaction. Whoever Putin has as his god or the equivalent needs a serious shakeup, and consideration given to moral injustice and integrity.

Some some serious outdoor philosophical travellers like to sit around an open fire looking at the flames for inspiration.

SITTING ON THE FENCE

Come sit down beside me
I said to myself,
And although it doesn't make
        sense,
I held my own hand
As a small sign of trust
And together I sat on the
        fence.

16
ROUTINES, TRADITIONS AND DEMOCRACY

"How is it possible to expect that mankind will take advice, when they will not so much as take a warning?" — Jonathan Swift

Observations of people's habits and behaviour. The freedom to enjoy the ridiculous, the traditional, the dog walking, and doing things 'just for the sake of them.' What I want, when I want. The beauty of life, looking at clouds, babies, antiques, Sunday markets. Doing things on occasion simply because I could.

For imagined slights or criticisms, get rid of retaliatory behaviour. Forget the old saying 'Don't get angry, get even!' When visiting wonderful pioneer museums all over the world and looking in awe at histories of battles and wars I can only wonder at past greed and envy. Human nature, of men in particular, has a serious flaw.

Western-style democracy breeds habits particularly in the area of creating personal wealth. Most of us, myself included, aspired to live on 'Prosperous Hill' mainly to have control over our own lives. But at what personal cost? I know the saying 'it's tough at the top' and have personally experienced all the usual benefits that go along with it, but it's also too easy to dismiss the downside of social snobbery, outright rudeness and downright ignorance and even cruelty to others, that many participants are too stupid to appreciate or even understand.

The 'silly season' (i.e., any extended holiday season) is long and over-tolerated simply because of positions in society or because of where they live. An 'entitlement' culture. It is absurd. Earn privileges! The corollary being 'Don't judge a book by its cover'.

Isn't it just great to see one of the best tennis players of all time (Nadal—sadly not playing much in 2023), still fidget and fiddle with his hair, his trousers, and avoiding walking on the lines. He is different and doesn't care.

A good reminder of happy poems; one about bears by AA Milne, *Lines and Squares*.

> Whenever I walk in a London Street
> I'm ever so careful to watch my feet
> And keep in the squares
> And the masses of bears,
> Who wait at the corners all ready to eat
> The sillies who tread on the lines of the street
> Go back to their lairs,
> And I say to them, 'Bears,
> Just look how I'm walking in all the squares!'
> And the little bears growl to each other, 'He's mine,
> As soon as he's silly and steps on a line.'
> And some of the bigger bears try to pretend

That they came round the corner to look for a friend;
And they try to pretend that nobody cares
Whether you walk on the lines or squares.
But only the sillies believe their talk;
It's ever so important how you walk
And its ever so jolly to call out, "Bears,
Just watch me walking in all the squares!"

If Nadal continues to play, long may he continue to win the French Tennis Open and others with his unique style and talent. He is no conformist.

Colours

They make life worthwhile. The colours of the spectrum should be noted and looked for. 'Virgins in bed give you odd reactions'. That's how I was taught as a young kid to remember the names; Violet Indigo Blue Green Yellow Orange Red.

How colourless life would be without them. Not even the wonderment of clouds could be a compensation for no colours in life.

There would be no 'yellow brick road', or '*Blue Bayou*'! Would we miss having no 'green fingers', or violet Violets, and I puzzle about Indigo. I know it has a connection with India and results from mixing blue with violet. But is it a basic? What on earth could we call oranges!

I really love the full colours of the spectrum.

HOW YOU WILL KNOW IF A PERSON (PERHAPS A POLITICIAN, A POLICEMAN, A PARTNER OR A PRIEST) IS CORRUPT.

you must study the duck.

you must play with the duck.
you must talk with the duck.

you must look deeply into the eyes of the duck

Then looking into the face of the person, how will you know if that person is corrupt?

you must know the ways of the duck.

you must look deeply into the eyes of the duck

17
WOMEN

"Men have sight; women insight." — Victor Hugo

The above is stating the bloody obvious to me. Men and women are so very different. Jay definitely has some super insight in some areas!

I am astonished that some parents are prepared to allow their children to want to change gender long before the children are mature enough to make such a decision. Such a big decision. I am not opposed to the medical, physiological and psychological changes that need to be considered when the differences need to be established or re-established. Deep thought, research and consideration is needed and should be mandatory before irreversible action is taken.

I always have been happy to recognise and enjoy the company of women, diverse as they may be! My own luck has been to be partnered by one of the 'quirky' ones, for over 40 years. Jay sure as hell is not perfect, but of course neither am I!

We both have exited smoothly out of commercial life to enjoy both Victoria and the warmer climate in Northern Queensland over winter. A real beach, relaxing, mindset while we are there.

Jay is the quintessential 'Melbourne Financial Adviser' and Company Director who loves the aura of being known as involved at board level in both profit and not-for-profit companies and of mixing primarily with other successful well qualified women at clubs and conferences.

Her expertise and involvement reached further, into educating and helping other women in their careers. Since retirement her relaxation is most recently the card game of bridge. Is it a 'game'? Some days she is on a high and some days very depressed. She no doubt will become more and more formidable as her expertise increases. Reminds me of my days in golf until it became too frustrating for my limited tolerance.

I personally think, with bridge, how can any human being have fun by playing with total concentration with a partner, against the opposition for over two/three hours at a time? That is totally beyond my comprehension. I guess chess is the same. But of course, I'm told it is not about fun; it can be very competitive. Quite intelligent people of both sexes get fanatically hooked. But smart people including medical experts recommend daily physical exercise.

Affairs; physical or mental. Of course, they have always existed for some, but how to weather the storm and come out the other side when they do occur is the real achievement.

My section on observations is mainly based on women in coffee shops and what appear to be mundane conversations. My growing maturity suggests there is a very valuable part of human relationships on display in this area every day.

In my lifetime, women have become much more competitive, more openly rivals, and opinionated.

"A lion amongst ladies is a most dreadful thing" — Shakespeare. How things have changed.

Sex

No book could be worthwhile without a section on sex. So here it is!

Suffice to say, I still enjoy the contemplation of it. I enjoy well-presented sex scenes in well-produced movies. The sex must be a progression from a warm relationship to a consensual agreement and is never rough or ugly.

My appreciation is for love being fun and producing feelings of enjoyment. I was very shy regarding sexual exploration when young. I always considered sex should be mutually respectful, tender, and an outward show and appreciation of where the relationship was at. No rough stuff or anger or a means to hurt someone. I have never been able to understand why sex could be used as a weapon. It's not a weapon. Genuine passion should never be hard to identify. I have been lucky to experience this.

It seems some modern behaviour requires being non-boring, rather than a height of companionship. I know where I stand. Of course, years ago I occasionally watched pornography and quickly considered it insincere, brutal and meaningless. There is a place in well done stories to include assault and rape but I avoid those as they can be alluded to without graphic portrayal of every moment.

Interesting, now, that my calm acceptance of my current physical constraints does not include ever having been considered greatly experimental or innovative in the areas of position, or endeavour. With hindsight was I too busy or just boring? Without doubt it was sexual drive, the consideration in middle age that I was 'missing out' on some unexplored areas of possibility, that led me to selfishly roam into external 'exotic' scenarios that were available at the time. I am aware of the damage that was done. The awareness of the meaning of soft, warm, deep love should never be overlooked. A relationship must always be worked on.

Do not try to convince me we are all born equal! It is just not so in reality. Women are not yet there! They will and must continue to strive for equality. So much poverty in the world leads to exploitation and lack of opportunities.

In Australia, we are closer to equal opportunity. But not even close to 100 per cent. The indigenous, and all with black or brown skins, illiterate immigrants, those with handicaps, physical (both mental and medical); all still face casual racism and bias. Chances yes, but opportunities are limited.

I have this sublime confidence (never put to the test) that I can pick the most impressive women by observing the way they walk. They walk with shoulders slightly back, a gap between their knees so they don't look knock-kneed, and what they wear looks especially chosen for them, their grooming is very good and they have a confidence appropriate to their location, i.e., at ease and a ready smile for all. They are noticeable and usually articulate. They have their own style.

87 NOT OUT

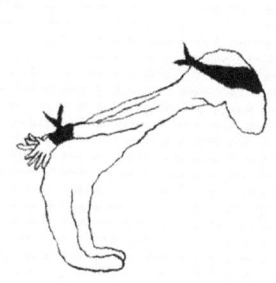

18
OWNERSHIP

"Love your neighbour, but don't pull down the hedge."
— Swiss proverb

What does anyone really 'own' in this world, and what does it mean too own stuff? How many and how much? Do collectors really own things, or are they just 'minding' them—'stewardship' as it's called.

You can't take it with you, all the things you think you own—so what's the point? I hear kids saying, "Dad, do we own this boat or that car?" They have not a clue what they are asking or saying. Does it matter? The answer, to many of my acquaintances, is that it does matter as they spend hours checking on the value of properties and shares to be able to inform all and sundry of how much they are worth. Added wealth becomes meaningless after a certain amount required to enjoy life in comfort.

Is personal ambition a factor in ownership of things, and is it just a part of active buying and selling—to make a profit to increase wealth and perceived happiness?

The most valuable things in my life, apart from family and friends, have only been properties and cars (and our super).

We have never accumulated very large amounts of capital or trust funds. Too much travelling and fun times over the years. As I start the downward slope of life, our homes and cars are still pretty much within my horizon. Is it a western thing?

Justification is sometimes difficult for me, but in the case of the houses, part of the reassurance is that that they are geographically well apart and the climate is so bad in Melbourne over winter! The cars are needed to get around, and one vehicle is five years old and the other eighteen years. Both homes are apartments and the beach one is used to create income when we are not there. Sometimes the coordination complications associated with the lifestyle are a bit much.

One of the happy results of luck in ownership in real estate has been as current owners in the holiday beach apartment in the Pullman Resort in Palm Cove, in far north Queensland. Was it Karma? We had a unit in Noosaville, some would no doubt call it Noosa, and after substantially upgrading it, we decided we were unhappy. Why? Noosaville had become too busy and noisy for us. Our small resort was also busy and noisy, and more than half the units were rent-outs, so were even more noisy. Some of the owners were real 'bogans', and the management was ineffectual. Most important of all we were cold! We even went out and bought electric blankets.

So, we went looking further north. The benefits attached to being associated with the Accor Group are outstanding and totally cooperative. We feel we have landed on our 'butts in honey'. I love being able to walk along the beach every day. The current management at the Pullman treat us almost like family.

Part of my lifestyle of keeping things simple. The main benefit should be able to sell them at short notice in the future, if and when needed. As my dad used to say, "We shall see what we shall see."

Relative to motor vehicles, all other things being equal, I consider the two vehicles currently owned are adequate and totally satisfy my ambitions. The newest and best is our Range Rover Evoque which we have owned from new and even though it uses 'dirty diesel', I have no plans to change it. The other car is a 2005 Jaguar S-Type in British Racing Green. It is special to me, and a little uncommon. Immaculate inside and out, and I am exploring if in time I can convert it to an electric. They are not exactly 'tin lizzie' wrecks.

A plan to give away or reduce some of what we own should be planned.

Travel

Over the past forty-plus years Jay and I have travelled widely. Early on much was business travel (conferences and the like) and then over the years we enjoyed many stays with friends, and later many overseas trips with friends; with the only exception of not ever visiting South America. So many other places and holidays were of our choice. Lucky to record all was good, with the minor exception of the loss of a bag or two—no disasters ever.

It is almost twenty years ago now since Specsavers took me to Guernsey, Hong Kong and China, and since then all my business trips have been within Australia. I truthfully don't miss any of it.

With the exception of one small board appointment; I am currently, 'a hero no more!'

"The pride of dying rich raises the laugh in hell." — John Foster

19
POLITICS

"Great is the good fortune of a state in which the citizens have a moderate and sufficient property." — Aristotle

I read widely and am very interested in local politics. When Jay suggested years ago that we perhaps buy a small property and move to France for six months every year, I was horrified because not speaking the local language I would not be able to understand the finer points of politics, culture, history and society. Rugby probably would have been OK!

For the first time in memory, I am optimistic that we in Australia, on a federal basis, have a government that is determined to reflect the will of 'the people' (ie as at January 2023).

That does not mean that the current Labor PM and team can ignore the past support base of working-class people and unions, but that they seem to be broad enough and collegiate enough to delegate properly to the team, and to also respect the opinions of women and the new group of Independent 'Teals' that reflects the pub test on many subjects. My hope also is that the Opposition Liberal Party will modify its political

Here **I** am...
UNEMPLOYED...
UNIMPORTANT...

And there **you** ARE...
WEALTHY....
POWERFUL...

HOW DO YOU SLEEP AT NIGHT...?

YOU OWN PROPERTY... GOLD... ART.... WINE AND HUMAN SOULS IN MASSIVE, SICKENING, CRIMINAL QUANTITIES...!

I sleep at night between silk sheets on a heated, king size auto-massage water bed with piped music in a very quiet street...

... with a companion whose beauty would make you weep with desire....

Leunig

Leunig

position and, more importantly, adjust its relationship with the outmoded far-right colleagues in the National Party. Perhaps a new middle of the road political party can evolve? And common sense prevails?

"*There is an infinity of political errors which, being once adopted become principles*" — Abbe Raynal.

The prime example is the policy on climate change. Fires and floods are enough to illustrate the power of nature, as is the beauty of whales doing their migratory annual voyages.

87 NOT OUT

The health of a democracy can be measured by its citizens ability to go into LOCKDOWN at short notice from the authorities.

But what is LOCKDOWN and how is it achieved?

TRue LOCKDOWN is a situation when every citizen is lying face down, rigid, motionless and obedient on the ground with eyes closed and making no sound whatsoever.

Great lockdowns are when citizens remain in the LOCKDOWN POSITION for up to three or four hours.

There is probably no sight more beautiful to a democratically elected leader than a city in FULL BLOWN LOCKDOWN.

LOCKDOWNS of up to thirteen hours have been achieved but that was when authorities had forgotten to give the all-clear signal.

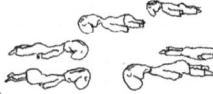

Leunig

20

THE NOW

"Everyone is perfectly willing to learn from unpleasant experience—if only the damage of the first lesson could be repaired." — Lichtenberg

This is about where I had thought to start my 'sneak' observations of human behaviour.

Sitting next to the beautiful swimming pool at our Palm Cove Resort in Queensland. The strident yells from kids, at the top of their voices…

"Dad, Dad! watch me! Dad, toss me in the air". Screams of uncontrolled delight…

"Again, Dad, again!" Perhaps because of the rarity of Dad playing with the children, 'Dad' is the call most commonly heard.

Poolside are two or three mothers in skimpy bikini swimmers, confessing to one another. "Bloody glad to see Henry helping for a change. He usually does bugger all. You know the kids have been driving me crazy. Mum does help, but Mum also drives me crazy!"

They all laugh together and admit they are so lucky. They

admit they don't quite know how they 'pulled' the luck thing, but hope it may last.

Do women still hope the old-fashioned joke will not apply to them? "Before marriage a man yearns for a woman. After marriage the 'Y' is silent".

As soon as one of the mothers walks off to help supervise the kids, the remaining mums can't resist a comment or two, "Doesn't she look great, but those tight black togs do exaggerate her bum."

The original idea for this book is not now so practical as my eavesdropping seems to intercept a much greater than anticipated use of the 'F and C' words, which I'm not that comfortable with. Why? It's just not my style.

I have decided on more humour and going back to ask, "Why... Why... Why...? About everything!

"Is life worth living? This is a question for an embryo not for an adult". – Samuel Butler.

Back to the subject of loneliness; my observations in coffee shops and cafes confirm what I have always thought. I handle most feelings of loneliness by realising I have kept myself isolated to a degree by personal choice.

I can spot 'suits' in luncheon areas who want to sit by themselves, just to enjoy their solitude and have a break. I can relate to that as it nearly always goes along with levels of leadership.

Another truism is the very old saying 'Little things mean a lot.' I think I learned a long time ago the value of that. A song by Anne Murray containing that lyric was an old favourite.

Now this next confession is going to surprise many who have known me for a long time. I have to remind my readers that I was sent to boarding school at a young age and that my mother in particular was a church-going Anglican. At school we, the boys, attended Sunday evening church by compulsion.

Even at a young age I was proclaiming rather grandiosely to be not an atheist, but an agnostic. I was not even all that sure what a 'pure Christian' was, but I was too lazy to investigate.

As an adult tourist, I have always enjoyed visits to churches of all sizes and beliefs in many different countries. I enjoy the singing of hymns that have rhythm even in foreign languages.

This little explanation above is to explain my choice of the lyrics and tune for my final words of song. I add that I have left out or minimised the word Lord and God, as inappropriate in my appreciation.

Count Your Blessings

When upon life's billows you are tempest-tossed
When you are discouraged, thinking all is lost,
Count your many blessings; name them one by one,
And it will surprise you what the Lord has done.

Are you ever burdened with a load of care?
Does the cross seem heavy you are called to bear?

Count your many blessings; ev'ry doubt will fly,
And you will be singing as the days go by.

When you look at others with their lands and gold,
Think that Christ has promised you his wealth untold
Count your many blessings; money cannot buy
Your reward in heaven nor your home on high.

(As an agnostic I ignore the words 'Christ' and 'Lord' but am OK with 'God' because most of us have some god-belief. It is the chorus that I often chant):

Count your blessings
Name them one by one
Count your blessings;
See what God hath done.
Count your blessings;
Name them one by one.
Count your many blessings;
See what God hath done.

It is a lovely conclusion and a lovely piece of music played by many famous musicians, soloists and choirs and composed by Johnson Oatman, Jr, in 1897 with the tune written by Edwin O. My message is "Be brave and optimistic."

Like Frank Sinatra singing *"Regrets, I've had a few..."* Better not to detail them, but some—I left too soon; not helping my children through their early adult years more; or even not having more children.

21
AMBITIONS

My Bucket List

Visit Milford Sound on a short cruise. Visit Lake Wanaka again.

Attend a first-class cricket match at the MCG.

Attend an All-Black's match at Eden Park.

Arrange a family get-together for either my 90th or 95th birthday. Include some friends!
Have suitable premises for a small dog.

Play in an Over 90s tennis tournament (anywhere).

Go to a Melbourne Cup on Members tickets.

Spend a day or two on Stewart Island eating oysters, with Shiraz.

'Give back' some more through a service group.

Not on the bucket list, but I'd like to study more about Egypt, the Romans and Japan.
My productivity has gone to hell but I am aiming to do another autobiographical musings book when I turn 95!
In amongst all of this I contemplate the difference between

Modern Stupid

It's much easier to go stupid these days than in previous times.

Now we can do it faster and with more comfort and convenience thanks to modern methods and technology.

Back in the old days they had to do it all by hand. It was sheer drudgery.

You can easily fit it into a busy life. It's available to everybody; right there at your fingertips.

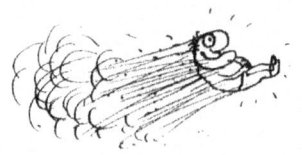

Leunig

me 'now' and just a year ago. As a follow-on from my original Autobiography completed in 2020, this has been a chance and an effort to look at life through different and older eyes. I hope these small musings illustrate it is possible to be contented and still contributing to society. I hope to be remembered as a decent person.

I have recently been to the 100th birthday celebration of a friend, then closely followed by her funeral. I looked at a baby in a pram at that 'celebration of life' (words chosen carefully for the funeral) and wondered what life in the future will be for that little baby. It's all very mind boggling.

Clearly at this age, my horizons are limited and regularly revised. My wisest philosophies are to be contented, to be generous in attitude, appreciate friends and retain a sense of humour. Staying positive! Stay decent and fair. Spend as much time as possible outdoors.

This book is not intended to be an admiration-seeking exercise, just an update of my own thoughts and musings. 'What's it all about?' is still a reasonable question. So, what is it really all about?

That's a pretty good question.

My final comment is how precious is "the privilege of freedom of thought": Respect how lucky we are.

WHY DO WE DO IT?
Nobody seems to know why we do it.

Nobody seems to even <u>ask</u> why we do it.

No voice of gentle inquiry. No bewildered cry from the street: the sudden shout, "Why do we do it?!"

How strange! It's as if everybody knows PRECISELY why we do it and the reason is too obvious to mention —

...or perhaps too vile and shameful to acknowledge; or too silly. Why the silence?

Do we do it because everybody else does it and because we're afraid of not doing it?
WHY? Please! Somebody!
WHY DO WE DO IT?

Leunig

The cartoons by Leunig throughout the book illustrate with humour how entertaining life can be.

My next writing project is another crime fiction/mystery book, probably called 'The Circus', again featuring Detective Linda Alexander and based in Melbourne.

www.ingramcontent.com/pod-product-compliance
Lightning Source LLC
Chambersburg PA
CBHW051539010526
44107CB00064B/2779